OVER 50,
Defined

Words just for us
that aren't
in the dictionary...

YET!

SHEL HARRINGTON

CREATOR OF
FAT-BOTTOM-FIFTIES GET FIERCE

D0802029

Fat-Bottom
FiftiesPress

For my mom, Yvette Abreu. At 95 years old she is still teaching me valuable lessons about life and relationships. The current lesson plan includes everything you ever wanted to know about aging: the good, the bad, the ugly, and the humor that can be found in the midst of it all.

Je t'aime maman. Je t'aime plus!!

OVER 50,
Defined

Words just for us
that aren't
in the dictionary . . .
YET!

iNTRODUCTiON

No matter how different we are, being over fifty unites us with a special bond. We've lived more than half a century – an amazing accomplishment!

We have joined a tribe that has interesting things going on with both our minds and our bodies (such as our bodies seem to have a mind of their own!). The problem is, we don't have a word to describe some of those special events. Sure, we can agree that some can be summarized as being a "senior moment," but that's the generalized term.

So what do you call it when you walk into a room, only to realize you have no idea why you went in? And what do you call that bathroom phenomenon? You know – the one where you pass a restroom knowing you don't have to go to the bathroom, but you decide to go in and use it anyways . . . just in *case* there's not one around when you need it? If you're over fifty, you know what I mean!

Quinbloits were made just for us. They are words that perfectly describe what is going on in our lives. Words that aren't in the dictionary . . . yet. From that weird turning down the car radio when we're lost so we can "see" better, to that two inch hair that sprouts out of our chin or ear while we sleep, there's a Quinbloit for that.

By the time you finish nodding and chuckling your way through this book, you'll know you're part of our tribe – we get you!

I bet you'll think of other situations that our over-fifty tribe can relate to that are crying out for a perfect Quinbloit of their own. When you do, please share them with me at quinbloit@gmail.com so we can properly name them and include them in the next Quinbloit collection.

QUINBLOIT | **kwin**-bloit (noun)
A unique word created to
describe an event, behavior,
or emotion people over fifty
universally experience.

NOTE: These words are not in
the dictionary . . . yet.

LET THE QUINBLOITS BEGIN!

ALWAFE | **awl**-weyf (noun)

That secure place you hide valuables so they'll always be safe, but then can't remember where it is.

Related term:

MUMMIFOOD | **muhm**-*uh*-food (noun)

That special treat you hid from your family in an alwafe that you stumble across six months later.

AARPIZE | **ahr**-pahyz (verb)

To transition from being offended by receiving the AARP magazine to looking forward to reading it.

Related term:

AARJUMP | **ahr**-juhmp (verb)

To immediately flip to the back of the AARP magazine to see what celebrities are hitting milestone birthdays.

BOFCABO | bof-**kab**-oh (verb)

To go to bed at the time you used to go out for the night.

Related term:

NORINGER | noh-**ring**-er (noun)

A person who goes to bed before midnight on New Year's Eve.

BEDJURY | **bed**-joor-ee (noun)

An injury sustained simply by getting out of bed.

Related terms:

BEDJURIOUS | bed-**joor**-e-*uh*s (adj)

Frequently sustaining mild injuries when getting out of bed or standing up from a sitting position. (See Riflop)

SNURIOUS | **snur**-ee-*uh*s (adj)

Having the ability to throw out your back, sprain a neck muscle, or slam your head into the object in front of you simply by sneezing.

BEDSTRACTION | bed-**strak**-sh*uh*n (noun)

The midday discovery that your bed is only half made because you got sidetracked by a ringing phone or the ping of an electronic device while making it.

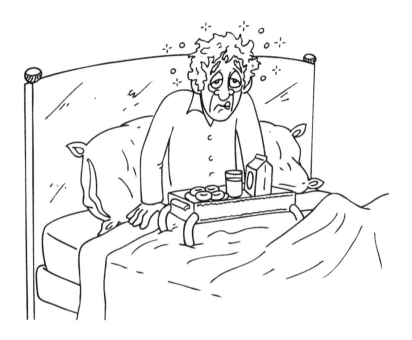

BLORMORT | **blohr**-mohrt (verb)

To wake up with that "morning after" feeling when you didn't have any alcohol or fun the night before.

BRISPER | **bris**-per (noun)

The whisper of hair that's left over each eye where eyebrows used to be.

Related term:

BROWNOUNCE | brou-**nouns** (noun)

Eyebrows that let the world know what color your gray hair used to be.

CALMBAT | **kahlm**-bat (noun)

The rage that builds up when someone tells you to "calm down."

Related term:

CALMBASTIC | kahlm-**bas**-tik

The intensified calmbat that results when, after being told to "calm down," the words "little missy" are added.

CATSPRISE | **cat**-sprahyz (noun)

The moment when, after waking up and chatting with your cat for five minutes, you put on your glasses and realize you've been talking to your slippers.

Related terms:

PETSPRISE | **pet**-sprahyz (noun)

When a catsprise happens with a pet that is not a cat.

TERRORSPRISE | **ter**-er-sprahyz (noun)

The moment for a petless person when, after waking up and screaming because of the large furry creature on their floor, they put on their glasses and realize they are afraid of their slippers.

CHISDOM | **chiz**-duhm (verb)

To call a grandchild to get instruction on how to use a new gadget.

COMPLUNK | kom-**pluhngk** (noun)

A compliment that is ruined by it ending with the words "for your age."

Examples:

You look great . . . for your age.

You can really dance . . . for your age.

CONDESNURT | con-duh-**snoort** (noun)

The annoyance felt when people decades younger than you call you sweetie, dear, or honey.

Related term:

DELUSASNURT | de-**loo**-zh*uh*-snoort (noun)

The annoyance felt when people close to your age and older call you Ma'am or Sir.

COUPSTUPE | **koop**-stupe (noun)

One who buys an item they wouldn't normally buy because it has a $2.00 off coupon that can be used at the checkout, then gets home and finds the unused coupon still attached to the product.

Related term:

Grashier | gra-**sheer** (noun)

The observant clerk at the checkout who spots a coupon attached to a product and asks the potential coupstupe if they'd like to use it.

DECALUSION | dek-uh-**loo**-zh*uh*n (noun)

The belief that "old" is always ten years older than your current age.

Related term:

SLODOTE | **sloh**-doht (noun)

The belief that getting old should take longer.

DRYJOE | **drahy**-joh (noun)

The disappointment felt when you go to pour your first cup of coffee, only to find you forgot to put water in the coffeemaker.

Related term:

CAFESPLOTTA | k*uh*-fey-**splot**-uh (noun)

The mess found in the morning when you forget to put the pot in the coffeemaker after you preset it the night before.

DOCMOCKED | **dok**-mokt (adj)

Having more than 50% of the names in your address book or contacts end in M.D.

Related term:

ADDRESAURAUS | ad-re-**sawr**-*uh*s (noun)

A person who still has an address book.

DOCSHOCK | **dok**-shok (verb)

To let out a gasp when you meet your new doctor and realize he or she is younger than your grandchild.

Related term:

DOCSHOCKQUASH | dok-shok-**quawsh** (noun)

The ability to squelch the urge to ask "Are you old enough to be a doctor?" immediately after you docshocked.

ENFLEPERY | en-**flep**-*uh*r-ee (noun)

The delusion that you don't need to write it down because you're sure you'll remember it.

Related term:

SCADPADOUS | skad-**pad**-us (adj.)

Having a pen and notepad in every room for those not afflicted with enflepery.

FASHFAIL | **fash**-feyl (noun)

The emotion experienced when the teenagers in your life ask to borrow some of your current wardrobe to wear so they can look retro.

FAUXPHORIA | foh-**fawr**-ee-uh (noun)

The momentary delight experienced when your loose pants indicate your weight loss efforts are paying off right before you realize your drawstring pants have come untied.

Related term:

FAUXSTRINGER | **foh-**string-er (noun)

A person who deliberately leaves their drawstring pants untied so they can have faux fauxphoria.

FILEBLIVION | fayhl-**bliv**-ee-*uh*n (noun)

An interesting tidbit you filed away so you could refer to it later, then forgot you did so.

Related term:

FILEBLITHER | fahl-**blith**-er (noun)

A file containing documents you can't remember why you saved.

FOGSLOG | **fog**-slog (verb)

To go to the store to buy an inexpensive item needed to complete a project, only to return home with numerous items – none of which is the item you went for.

Example:

While making cookies you realize you have no brown sugar. You go to the store to obtain the $3.00 item so you can finish your cookies. Two hours later you return home with $122.34 worth of groceries – and no brown sugar.

FOLLIGRATION | fol-i-**grey**-sh*uh*n (noun)

Hair growth that moves from one part of the body to another.

FORTUDUMB | fawr-ch**uh**-duhm (noun)

The age range wherein one has lived so long none of the stupid stuff they did was posted online.

FROBOP | **froh**-bop (verb)

To attempt to use the TV remote to make a
call, or your cell phone to change the
channel on the TV.

GARFABBLE | **gahr-**fab-*uh*l (verb)

To make random conversation with strangers at the grocery store.

Related terms:

GARFABBLER | **gahr**-fab-bler (noun)

An individual who can garfabble.

GARFABBLED | gar-**fab**-buld (adj)

Describes the result of one interacting with a garfabbler when they were not in the mood to garfabble.

GEEZOPT | **gee**-zopt (verb)

To choose between two or more social events based on which one will get you home earliest.

GERIPROVEMENT | je-ree-**proov**-m*uh*nt
(noun)

Additions to a home that involve amenities
such as grab bars and shower chairs.

GIFTCODGE | **gift**-koj (noun)

A stockpile of funny cards about being old and gift books with titles like *Over 50, Defined* one has on hand for unexpected gift-giving occasions because they are appropriate for any individual in their social circle.

GLOST | glawst (verb)

To look for your glasses when they're on your head or around your neck.

Related terms:

KLOST | klawst (verb)

To look for your car keys while holding them.

PHLOST | flost (verb)

To look for your phone while talking on it.

GRONIKER | **grawn**-i-ker (noun)

A name chosen, after an extensive search, to be used as an alternative to "grandma" or "grandpa."

Example:

You Google the words "grandmother" and "grandma," reviewing all their synonyms, and do not find something that reflects your youthful spirit. You then look up the word "grandmother" in every language that is remotely related to the heritage of you, your spouse, your child's mate, and the people who owned your home before you. Still finding nothing with enough panache to properly represent your new status, you interview all your grandparent friends to see what their grandchildren call them. You finally settle on the word "Chickie" because it is so darn cute.

HALLMUG | **hawl**-muhg (verb)

To reach the place in life where you buy more sympathy cards than birthday cards.

HAPZIZZER | hap-**ziz**-er (noun)

A person who resented required naps as a child who now takes naps without being told and refers to each as "happy hour."

INJUNKLE | in-**juhngk**-*uh*l (verb)

To read cooking instructions on the food box, confidently throw it away, then retrieve it from the trash seconds later to recheck the instructions.

Related term:

INJUNKIE | in-**juhngk**-ee (noun)

One who injunkles multiple times with the same box.

JARMENTIME | **jahr**-men-tahym (noun)

That place in life where participating in "contact sports" means contacting your friends to play shuffleboard or throw darts.

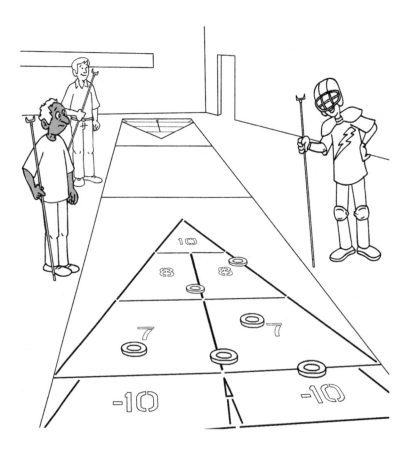

JAVANUKE | **jah**-vuh-nyook (noun)

The cold cup of coffee you discover in the microwave hours after you popped it in for a quick re-heat.

JIGGELBITZ | **jig**-uhl-bitz (noun)

The ongoing movement that occurs when you come to a sudden stop and parts of your body don't.

JOINTOLOGIST | joint-**ol**-*uh*-jist (noun)

One whose joints predict weather more accurately than meteorologists do.

LIQUEND | li-**kwend** (noun)

The time of day when you stop drinking liquids before going to bed to avoid the need to get up in the night. (See Plibble)

MINTCESSITY | mint-**ses**-i-tee (noun)

The need to always have breath mints within reach during social encounters.

Related term:

MINTASTROPHE | min-**tas**-truh-fee (noun)

After eating garlic, onion, or tuna fish at a social event, you find your mint container empty.

NEBATE | ne-**beyt** (verb)

To have an internal debate as to whether or not you need what you dropped on the floor enough to exert the energy necessary to bend over and pick it up.

NITENUMS | **nahyt**-nuhmz (noun)

Bedtime snacks that consist of Extra Strength Tums or Advil. Or both.

NOSTALJURK | nu-**stawl**-jurk (noun)

A person who has started more than six sentences with "I remember when . . ." within a three day period.

OBITCHECK | oh-**bit**-chek (verb)

To read obituaries to see how long people are living instead of to find out who died.

OHYAH | oh-**yah** (verb)

To come up with the perfect retort two days after the argument.

OOFFIT | **oof**-fit (noun)

The noise you now make when getting up from a sitting position.

OTICSIGHT | **o**-tik-sahyt (verb)

To turn down the volume on the car radio when you are lost so you can see better.

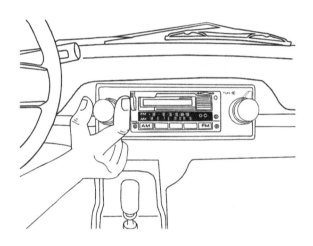

PEEYOP | **pe**-yop (noun)

The use of a bathroom just because you're passing it – in case there's not one close by when you need it.

Related term:

MISTPEEYOP | **mist**-pee-op (noun)

On the highway, spotting a bathroom after you have passed it and it's too late to stop.

PILLIGATION | pil-li-**gey**-sh*uh*n (noun)

The act of filling up one's pillbox for the
week – generally performed on a Sunday
evening.

Related term:

TRIPILLIGATION | **trayh**-pil-li-**gey**-sh*uh*n (noun)

The term used when the pillbox has three rows for those who take pills three times a day.

MINIPHARMPILLIGATION | min-ee-**fahrm**-pil-li-**gey**-sh*uh*n (verb)

To fill anything larger than a tripilligation.

PLIBBLE | **plib**-buhl (verb)

To blearily trudge to the bathroom to pee while attempting to continue sleeping.

Related terms:

PLIBPRIDE | **plib**-prahyd (noun)

The realization you made it through an
entire night without needing to plibble.

PLIBGAB | **plib**-gab (noun)

A conversation wherein participants
discuss how many times they plibbled in
a given night or claim plibpride.

PLIPLO | **plip**-loh (noun)

That awkward moment when a voice answers the phone and you can't remember who you called.

PLUGOOPS | plug-**oops** (noun)

The hour of frustration you spent trying to make an electric appliance or electronic device work, only to find out it's not plugged in.

POFNITO | pof-**nee**-toh (verb)

To stay in your pajamas so long after getting up that there is no point getting dressed because it's almost time to go back to bed.

Related term:

PREJAY | **pree**-jey (verb)

To change into pajamas when you get home from work or an outing, even though bed time is hours away, to avoid the need to change twice.

POLITESMITE | p*uh*-**lahyt**-smahyt (noun)

The reality check experienced as a result of holding open the door for an old person, then realizing you went to high school with them.

PUNSTUN | **puhn**-stuhn (noun)

That period of time when you go from making fun of cheesy puns to actually making cheesy puns.

QUEATHTAB | **kweeth**-tab (verb)

To label your furniture and belongings based on who is going to get it after you're gone.

QUIBBY | **kwib**-ee (noun)

A universal greeting to mask the fact you can't remember someone's name – as in "Hey there ... buddy. Great to see you."

Related term:

QUIBBEE | **kwib-**ee (noun)

The recipient of a quibby because the speaker (regardless of how many times he has met you) can't remember your name.

QUINBLOIT | **kwin**-bloit (noun)

A unique word created to describe an event, behavior, or emotion people over fifty universally experience.

NOTE: These words are not in the dictionary ... yet.

QUINBLOIT | **kwin**-bloit (verb)

To create a unique word to describe an event, behavior, or emotion people over fifty universally experience.

REPITEDUM | rep-i-**tee**-duhm (noun)

When friends and family correct the details of a story you're telling because they've heard it so many times.

RIFLOP | **rahy**-flop (verb)

To roll around before you are able to get up from a sitting position on the floor.

Related term:

RIFLOPLUSION | ri-floh-**ploo**-sh*uh*n (noun)

The mistaken belief that you can get up from a sitting position on the floor without riflopping.

ROOMEMBER | roo-**mem**-ber (verb)

To stand in the middle of a room while trying to remember why you went in it.

Related term:

BLOTZWALK | **blots**-wawk (verb)

To retrace your steps until something triggers the reason you entered the room.

NOTE: When the memory is triggered, you should immediately write it down before heading back to the location where you previously roomembered.

SACKSTASHER | **sak**-stash-er (noun)

One who keeps a bag of bags in the pantry.

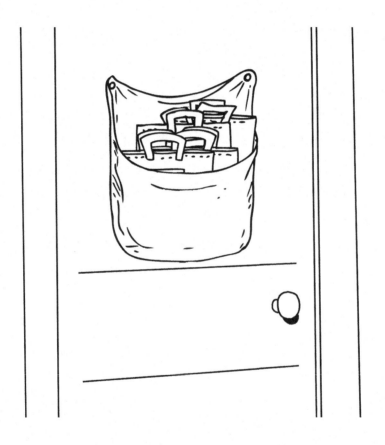

Related term:

BOXSTOCKER | **boks**-stok-er (noun)

One who saves unneeded cardboard boxes because they are "good boxes."

SADHILATION | sad-hi-**ley**-sh*uh*n (noun)

The act of sucking in your stomach with little or no change of appearance.

SENIORSUMPTION | seen-yer-**suhmp**-sh*uh*n (noun)

A clerk's assumption you qualify for a senior discount just by looking at you.

Related term:

SENIORUMBRAGE | seen-yer-**uhm**-brij (noun)

The indignation you feel when someone makes a seniorsumption about you – no matter how many years you have actually qualified for the senior discount.

SKLIMP | **sklimp** (noun)

Finally having the time to sleep in, but the inability to do so.

Related term:

CLARM – **klarm** (noun)

The cat wails, pounces on you, and stares at your closed eyes until you get up to feed him at the time your alarm *used* to go off.

SKLOPS | **sklops** (noun)

Ugly shoes that are so comfortable you don't care how ugly they are.

SLAPDAP | **slap**-dap (verb)

To pull together an outfit from your closet based on what still fits.

SPAZTASK | **spaz**-task (noun)

A consecutive series of tasks executed as a result of a distraction encountered during the first task and each task thereafter until the initial task is remembered and completed.

Example:

While emptying the dishwasher you put away a bowl and notice that there is a crack in another bowl, so you throw the cracked bowl in the trash and smell something foul, so you take the garbage bag outside to the bins and decide to get the mail from the mailbox while you're outside, then on your way back to the house you see a patch of weeds in your flower bed that you spend the next twenty minutes pulling out. You go into the house to wash the dirt off your hands and see that the dishwasher is only half emptied, which results in you having to decide whether to finish the original task or go retrieve the mail from the place you set it next to the flowerbed and potentially extend the length of the spaztask.

SPAZTASK | **spaz**-task (verb)

To execute a spaztask.

Related term:

SPAZTASKER | **spaz**-task-er (noun)

A person who is prone to spaztasking.

74

SUNSPROCKS | **suhn**-sproks (noun)

Apparel, such as hats and sunglasses, that are selected based on the level of protection it affords rather than the fashion statement it makes.

TADONE | t*uh*- **duhn** (noun)

The accomplished feeling you get after writing a to-do list.

NOTE: If you put "write to-do list" on your list, you get to cross something off immediately for an instant tadone!

TELECODGER | tel-*uh*-**koj**-er (noun)

A person with first-hand knowledge of telephone related terms such as party line, dial up, and busy signal.

Related terms:

TELEBANGER | **tel**-*uh*-bang-er (noun)

A person who has experienced the immense satisfaction of ending an unpleasant phone call by slamming the receiver down on its base.

TELEWONKER | **tel**-*uh*-wongk-er (noun)

A person who has experienced the frustration of having to stay home if they were waiting for an important call.

TEXTELL | **tekst**-tel (verb)

To make it obvious you are old by using complete sentences and punctuation when you are texting.

TIMELASTIC | tahym-**las**-tik (noun)

When terms such as "recently," "not long ago," and "a few years back" refer to an event that took place double-digit years ago.

TRAVELGEEZER | **tra**-v*uhl*-gee-zer (noun)

One whose suitcase, after being packed for a two-week trip, contains more medications and toiletries than clothes.

TRESSTRESS | **tres**-stress (verb)

To notice the first gray hair . . . on your child.

UNSCRUFF | **uhn**-skruhf (noun)

A haircut that includes eyebrows and ears.

WAMBONGER | **wam**-bawng-ger (noun)

A person who remembers starting every Saturday morning by watching cartoons.

WEWATCH | **wee**-woch (verb)

To look at your watch three times before you actually remember what time it is.

Related term:

DUHDATE | duh-**deyt** (verb)

To look at the date on a calendar three times before you actually remember what the date is.

ZAPSMACK | **zap**-smak (verb)

To receive a shock when you look in the mirror and see someone at least twenty years older than you were expecting.

ACKNOWLEDGEMENTS

This book has been in-the-making since 2015 when I first published a Quinbloits post on my *Fat-Bottom-Fifties Get Fierce* blog. Numerous conversations with friends and other over 50s in the years since highlighted how many of the jarring events and phenomena of the aging process are universal, but we don't have anything to call them. I decided each should have its own Quinbloit – so we could have our own little dictionary of words that would spare us the need for lengthy explanations. I would like to thank all those who helped me take this fun from blog post to book.

For praying for me and this project, as well as doing an early review and giving me feedback, thank you Natine Abreu-Shaw, Laura Bentley, and Gene and Lou Christian. And a very special thanks to Dee Dee Chumley for painstakingly going through each definition and lovingly challenging me on all things grammar. (She'll appreciate the irony of two adverbs appearing in the sentence that thanks her – I'm pretty sure I can hear her cringing.) Dee Dee also contributed a bonus quinbloit (see Folligration).

To my BFF for over four decades, Margaret (Mag-B) Mrdeza, for conceiving the *Fat-Bottom-Fifties Get Fierce* idea with me with our early joint blog and the collaborations since.

For all the brainstorming, feedback, prayer and support, big thanks to my 2717 MasterMind team (iron does, indeed, sharpen iron!), Rene Gutteridge, Christy Johnson, Marci Seither, Gena Maselli, and Christopher Maselli. Special thanks to Chris – from early encouragement (some might say "pushing") to the hands-on help throughout the publishing process, this book would literally not be here without his assistance.

For being the "light of my life and my reason for living" for over 40 years, and for standing by me through thick and thin (even though it was mostly thick!), thanks to my husband, Steve. I can't imagine anybody better to spend my quinbloiting years with!

And last, but definitely not least, a big shout-out and thank you to my Facebook and website *Fat-Bottom-Fifties Get Fierce* tribe for all the inspiration, laughs, and community you have contributed for the past seven years – you are my people!

ABOUT THE AUTHOR

Shel Harrington is a humorist who writes for a (chronologically!) mature audience at FatBottomFiftiesGetFierce.com and has over 475,000 followers on her smile-inducing *Fat-Bottom-Fifties Get Fierce Facebook page*.

In her alternative life, Shel is a seasoned Family Law attorney who writes and speaks about how to put her out of business by doing marriage better.

Shel and her husband, Steve, live in Oklahoma on a little plot of earth called *Dragonroost* with their two cats, Moxie and Homer. Shel would like to claim that Homer was named after the author of classic literature, but she's pretty sure that when Steve insisted if they were going to have two cats he got to name one, he wasn't thinking about the *Iliad* or the *Odyssey* when he made his choice.

Contact Shel at quinbloit@gmail.com.

HAVE A GREAT iDEA FOR A QUiNBLOiT?

Email it to quinbloit@gmail.com
for a chance to have it included
(with credit to you, of course!)
in the next Quinbloit collection.

LET'S STAY CONNECTED!

Stay connected with Shel and the gang at
Fat-Bottom Fifties Get Fierce by signing up for
the newsletter at
FatBottomFiftiesGetFierce.com

You can also join us on social media at:

Facebook.com/FatBottomFiftiesGetFierce

Twitter.com/FatBottom50s

Pinterest.com/FatBottomFiftie

THANK YOU

Thank you for quinbloiting with us.

If *Over 50, Defined* made you smile, I really would appreciate it if you would write a short review. It really does make such a difference!

Shel Harrington

Made in the USA
Columbia, SC
06 May 2021